THE CUTTING EDGE

WEAPONS

Bigger, Stronger, and Smarter

Mark Morris

Heinemann Library
Chicago, Illinois

Designed by Richard Parker and Tinstar Design www.tinstar.co.uk
Printed and bound in China by South China Printing Company

10 09 08 07 06
10 9 8 7 6 5 4 3 2 1

Library of Congress Cataloging-in-Publication Data

Morris, Mark.
  Weapons / Mark Morris.
      p. cm. -- (The cutting edge)
  Includes bibliographical references and index.
  ISBN 1-4034-7430-3 (library binding-hardcover) -- ISBN 1-4034-7436-2 (pbk.)
  1. Weapons--Juvenile literature. I. Title. II. Cutting edge (Chicago, Ill.)
  U800.M58 2007
  623.4--dc22
                              2005018020

Acknowledgements
The author and publishers are grateful to the following for permission to reproduce copyright material: Colt p. 6; Corbis pp. 4–5, 14, 24, 26, 27, 29, 30, 33, 41, 43, 44, 45, 46, 47; Courtesy of Trekaerospace.com p. 35; Defence Picture Library pp. 19, 23, 37, 39; Getty pp. 51; Military Picture Library pp. 17 (Yves Debay), 21 (Alexi Grachtchenkov), 11 (Geoff Lee), 8, 15 (Peter Russell), 7 (Hugh Threlfall); Science Photo Library p. 49; TRH pp. 20, 22, 34;

Cover photograph of a Joint Strike Fighter X-35C, reproduced with permission of Lockheed Martin/Getty.

Illustrations by Jeff Edwards.

Our thanks to Mark Adamic for his assistance in the preparation of this book.

Every effort has been made to contact copyright holders of any material reproduced in this book. Any omissions will be rectified in subsequent printings if notice is given to the publishers.

The paper used to print this book comes from sustainable resources.

Contents

Some words in the book are in bold, **like this**. You can find out what they mean by looking in the glossary.

Weapons Through the Ages

History shows that successful armies have two things in common: better **tactics** and better weapons. Without one of these, and often without both, victory in battle is unlikely. Having the best weapons is always an advantage.

The ancient Romans had advanced ways of producing metal for their swords. This meant the swords were less likely to shatter when used in combat. It gave the Romans the edge in battle.

In the Middle Ages, the longbow became the weapon every army wanted. Arrows could be shot accurately over greater distances with more power. For many years, it was this weapon that gave an army the advantage.

The invention of gunpowder led to many further advances. Weapons could be fired over greater distances, and this new explosive power changed the way battles were fought.

For centuries, the power of the British Empire was built on the power of its navy. The British Navy built the best sailing ships with the heaviest **armament**, and so it ruled the waves.

The invention of the machine gun had a huge effect on World War I. Up until this time, an army had to have a greater number of troops to win a battle. The machine gun meant that a very small number of soldiers could cause extraordinary damage because of increased firepower.

World War I also saw the arrival of the armored vehicle, or tank. These tanks were not advanced, and there were not enough of them to dramatically change the course of the war. But they changed the way that future ground battles would be fought.

Air power became all-important during World War II. At the start of the war, Adolf Hitler's use of the Stuka dive-bomber allowed him to cut through enemy lines with great power and speed. Later in the war, it was the **Allies'** superior aircraft, such as the Spitfire and the Hurricane, that turned the tide of battle in their favor.

Since the 1950s, nuclear missiles have been the most important kind of weapon. They are very different from all previous weapons because they have very rarely been used. Yet just having nuclear weapons is enough to make sure enemies stay away. Linked to the importance of nuclear weapons is the submarine. Being able to silently launch your missile from under water, off the coast of an enemy, is a great tactical advantage.

All the examples on this page are examples of "cutting-edge" weaponry throughout history. But what would be considered a "cutting-edge" weapon today?

Having better weapons and tactics means the enemy is likely to be defeated.

Infantry Weapons

Firearms

The handgun does not win battles, but it saves the lives of those fighting in the battle. To those on the battlefield, their pistols may be all that is going to protect them.

So, what are the important requirements of an outstanding handgun? Power? Accuracy? **Magazine** size? Soldiers will tell you all of these are important, but not as important as reliability. Battered against rocks, choked with sand, dropped underwater, a soldier needs to know that his or her handgun is going to work.

Old Faithful

The Colt M1911 .45 pistol is the greatest handgun of all time. Its operation system has been copied so widely that it is still the blueprint for most new pistols today.

This weapon was used in World War I. It was then in service until it was finally replaced in 1985 as the standard pistol for the U.S. Army. This caused a storm of protest from soldiers, but the Army wanted to use a 9-millimeter (mm) weapon with a larger magazine capacity. Most soldiers disagreed and wanted to stick with "Old Faithful", the weapon that never let them down.

Colt .45 M1911 pistol

Caliber:	0.45 in.
Magazine:	7 rounds
Weight:	2.49 lbs. empty, 3.0 lbs. loaded
Length:	8.6 in. (21.9 cm)
Muzzle velocity:	830 ft. (253 m) per second

The guerrilla gun

The AK-47, designed by Mikhail Kalashnikov, is the most successful assault rifle ever made. If all the different types are included, over 50 million have been produced. For over 40 years, this famous rifle armed Soviet **infantrymen**. It has also become the chosen weapon for **guerrilla** and terrorist operations.

The AK-47's design is simple, effective, and virtually idiot-proof. It can be dropped in mud or sand, and it can fire thousands of **rounds** without the need for cleaning. Almost anyone can be taught to use it.

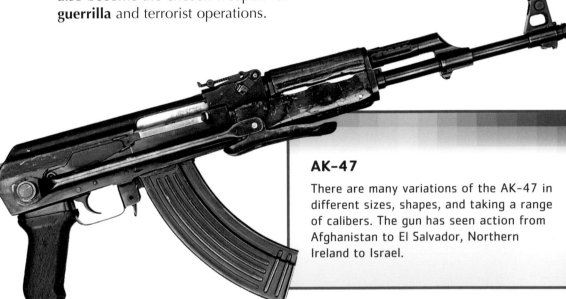

AK–47

There are many variations of the AK–47 in different sizes, shapes, and taking a range of calibers. The gun has seen action from Afghanistan to El Salvador, Northern Ireland to Israel.

The key features that make this weapon so successful are:

- Reliability: The simple design means that even very poorly maintained rifles still work.

- Firepower: Guerrilla armies rarely have marksmen (people skilled at hitting targets). The AK-47 releases many shots in the general direction of the target.

This increases the chance of hitting it.

- **Bayonet**: It is one of the few modern weapons to have a bayonet attachment. The wooden butt also makes it effective as a club.

- Build: The wooden exterior looks cheap, but is actually very well built. It can handle a severe battering and still work.

The sniper rifle

A sniper, a person who shoots from a concealed location, uses a rifle that has a far greater range than those carried by ordinary troops. This makes skillful snipers the most dangerous people on a battlefield. They remain unseen as they fire at targets from great distances.

There are many weapons that could claim to be the best sniper's rifle, but the British M85 is about as accurate a rifle as it is possible to build. It was originally designed as a rifle for shooting competitions, but it is now used by armies and police forces worldwide.

The M85 has a silent safety catch and a rubber shoulder pad to cope with the weapon's enormous **recoil**. A good marksman can hit a target the size of a quarter from about 0.5 miles (600 to 700 meters) away. A good sniper is expected to be able to hit a person from this distance. Depending on the **ammunition** being used, the rifle can pierce targets, such as light tanks or helicopters, or it can even set targets on fire.

Night vision

Telescopic sights (devices that help the eye aim on a faraway object) have given snipers greater accuracy for years—but what about at night?

An infrared sight is a device that forms an image using infrared **radiation**. This is similar to the way a normal camera forms an image using light. Objects always give off a certain amount of radiation. Generally speaking, objects that are hot by human standards give off more infrared radiation than those that are cold. This radiation can be detected in a similar way to how a normal camera detects visible light. An infrared sight normally shows hot areas as white and cool objects as black. Since it picks up infrared and not light, it can work in total darkness.

Laser sights

Laser sights are often seen in Hollywood movies. Unfortunately, they are an example of complex technology being less effective than what it was designed to replace. A laser projects a red dot onto a target that can be seen through conventional telescopic sights. But it does not work very well in bright light (such as a sunny day), since the light makes it harder to see the laser dot. The red dot can also reveal the position of the sniper to the enemy. In effect, a laser sight is similar to waving a flashlight at the enemy! There are now infrared laser sights that project a dot that can only be seen through special equipment. But the enemy often has night vision equipment, too!

M85 sniper rifle

Cartridge:	7.62 mm
Magazine:	10 rounds
Weight:	12.6 lbs. (with telescopic sight)
Length:	45.3 in. (115 cm)

Rapid fire

The machine gun changed the battlefield forever. Where soldiers once had to reload after a single shot, they could now fire hundreds of rounds per minute without a single pause.

It is surprising how simple machine guns actually are. These weapons are certainly examples of precision engineering, but they operate on some very basic concepts.

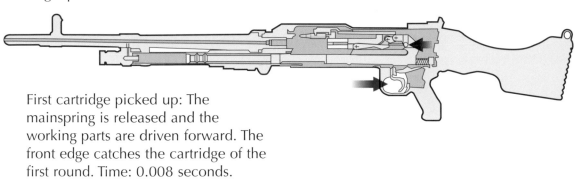

First cartridge picked up: The mainspring is released and the working parts are driven forward. The front edge catches the cartridge of the first round. Time: 0.008 seconds.

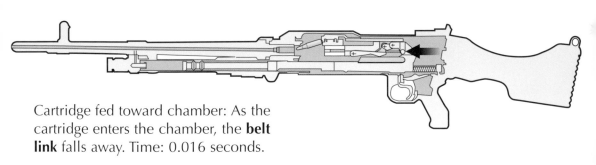

Cartridge fed toward chamber: As the cartridge enters the chamber, the **belt link** falls away. Time: 0.016 seconds.

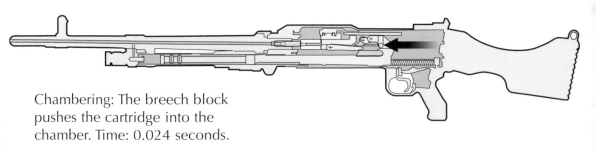

Chambering: The breech block pushes the cartridge into the chamber. Time: 0.024 seconds.

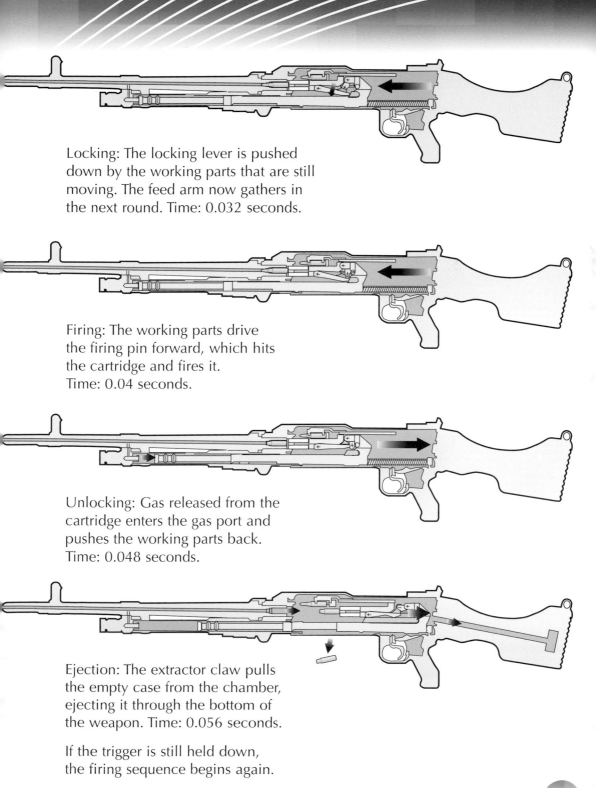

Locking: The locking lever is pushed down by the working parts that are still moving. The feed arm now gathers in the next round. Time: 0.032 seconds.

Firing: The working parts drive the firing pin forward, which hits the cartridge and fires it. Time: 0.04 seconds.

Unlocking: Gas released from the cartridge enters the gas port and pushes the working parts back. Time: 0.048 seconds.

Ejection: The extractor claw pulls the empty case from the chamber, ejecting it through the bottom of the weapon. Time: 0.056 seconds.

If the trigger is still held down, the firing sequence begins again.

Submachine guns

Small, cheap, and easily hidden, the submachine gun is the main anti-terrorist weapon. It provides the maximum amount of short-range firepower in a tiny package. Since submachine guns are small and easy to carry, the police carry them at airports and the president's bodyguards keep theirs hidden away.

Professional soldiers argue that there is no military role for submachine guns today. They are great for spraying bullets—as long as you do not mind where they hit. But these weapons have found a new battlefield: crime and terrorism.

The Heckler and Koch MP5 is the most widely used submachine gun. The MP5 is not a simple gun to use or maintain. It is more complex and more expensive than other submachine guns. But in the hands of an expert, it is far safer and much more accurate than other submachine guns. This is why the MP5 is overwhelmingly the weapon of choice for elite rescue teams and special operations units.

Heckler and Koch MP5

Caliber:	9 mm
Weight:	6.4 lbs. (loaded with full magazine)
Length:	26.8 in. (68 cm)
Muzzle velocity:	925 ft. (282 m) per second
Rate of fire:	800 rounds per minute

Ammunition

An infantry weapon is useless without ammunition. There are many different types of ammunition to choose from. Not only do they vary in size, but different ammunition will have a different effect on a target. A lot of research and investigation has been carried out into the effects of bullets. Even so, there is no foolproof way to predict how deadly a particular round will be.

If the bullet is traveling at extremely high speed, and if it is pointed and hard, it will tend to pass through a material and still maintain high speed and energy. The shock wave in front of the bullet, and the suction caused behind it by its rapid speed, can cause great damage. If the speed is not so great, a pointed, hard bullet tends to pass through the target without causing so much damage. This means that most "assault rifle" bullets do relatively little damage to a person, providing that they go through flesh and miss major organs.

A flattened bullet is more likely to expand and shatter on impact. This causes major damage.

Different types of small arms ammunition

Full Metal Jacket (FMJ) Solid lead surrounded by strong casing. Unlikely to break up and goes deeply into target.

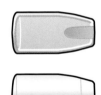

Semi-Jacketed Hollow Point (SJHP) Expands more quickly than the JHP.

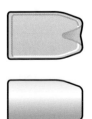

Jacketed Hollow Point (JHP) A hole at the tip ensures the bullet expands quickly when hitting the target. This causes greater damage. Highly accurate.

Soft Point (SP) The lead tip is exposed. This means there is maximum expansion when the bullet hits the target, spreading the damaged area.

Tanks

Caterpillar track is the common name for the endless flexible belt of metal plates on which tanks move. Caterpillar tracks work in the same way as a conveyer belt in a factory. Within the moving track, the tank's wheels ride along just as the wheels in a car run along the road. The tank has a track on each side. So, in order to turn, the tank's engine drives small cogwheels that turn the track.

> It is the ability to go virtually anywhere that makes a tank so dangerous on the battlefield.

The advantages of tracks

The advantages of tracks include:

- Greater grip (especially in slippery conditions such as mud or snow)

- Low pressure on the ground and high **flotation,** so vehicles are less likely to sink into the ground and get stuck.

Tracked vehicles can move quickly and easily over difficult ground because the track makes contact with a wide area of ground. A car grips the ground with only the bottom part of its tires, but a tank grips with a much greater area of track. Additionally, the track has a heavy **tread** that digs into muddy surfaces. It also never goes flat, as a tire can. Although this cutting-edge technology is a century old, it has never been improved upon.

Challenger 2 Battle Tank

Crew:	4
Length:	37.9 ft. (11.55 m)
Height:	8.17 ft. (2.49 m)
Combat weight:	68.9 tons (62.5 tonnes)
Main armament:	1 x 120-mm L30 CHARM Gun
Secondary armament:	Co-axial 7.62-mm chain gun; 7.62-mm GPMG Turret-Mounted Gun
Engine	1200 hp Perkins-Condor CV12
Maximum road speed:	37 mph (59 km/h)
Average cross-country speed:	25 mph (40 km/h)

Up for the challenge

The Challenger tank had already established itself as an outstanding weapon, but over 150 improvements make the Challenger 2 even more unstoppable.

A completely new power unit, better **suspension**, and improved tracks have been added. Smoke grenade launchers have been fitted to the **turret**. Smoke can also be produced by injecting diesel fuel into the engine exhausts. The smoke pumps out of the tank, providing **camouflage**. The all-new turret has an improved 120-mm L30A1 rifled cannon, which

fires the new DU (depleted uranium) round. An L37A2 7.62-mm machine gun is mounted on the turret, and a Boeing L94A1 7.62-mm **chain gun** is also installed. The turret is protected with improved armor. It also has a nuclear, biological, and chemical (NBC) protection system. The **fire control system** uses the most sophisticated computer available. The laser range-finder has an accurate range up to 6.2 miles (10 kilometers).

With all these improvements, the Challenger 2 is not a weapon to be taken lightly.

The awesome Abrams

The M1A2 Abrams tank uses its high mobility, incredible firepower, and shock effect to destroy enemy forces on the battlefield. It has a 120-mm main gun, a powerful 1,500 horsepower (hp) turbine engine, and special armor. These make the Abrams an excellent choice for attacking or defending against large numbers of heavily armored forces on a highly deadly battlefield. Many experts believe it is the finest tank ever produced.

The Abrams tank has an extremely powerful cannon combined with very tough armor that makes the tank hard to destroy when a shot hits the front.

The biggest advantage the Abrams has is its ability to accurately hit enemy tanks at extremely long range. Over open ground, such as a desert battlefield, it can engage and destroy just about any other tank in the world before another tank can get close enough to fire. This range advantage comes from **optics** and computer fire control systems that other tanks have never been able to match.

The mission of the Abrams is simple: close in on an enemy with superior speed and destroy using superior firepower.

⚔ Make the connection

Tank designers are constantly looking for ways to improve the Abrams tank. It is being given greater armor protection, improvements to the suspension, and a nuclear, biological, and chemical (NBC) protection system that increases the crew's chances of survival in a **contaminated** environment. Recently, a commander's **thermal viewer** has been installed, and the commander's weapon station and fire control systems have been improved.

Abrams Battle Tank—M1A2

Length:	32 ft. (9.76 m)	Armament:	1 x 120-mm M256 smoothbore gun
Width:	12 ft. (3.65 m)		1 x 12.7-mm machine gun
Height:	8 ft. (2.44 m)		1 x 7.62-mm machine gun
Top speed:	42 mph (67 km/h)		1 x 7.62-mm machine gun on a **skate mount**
Weight:	67.8 tons (61.5 tonnes)		6 x smoke grenade launchers
Crew:	4	Range:	300 mi. (483 km)

The main disadvantage of all tanks is their weight and fuel needs. The Abrams tank can only go about 1 mile (1.6 kilometers) on 3 gallons (11.4 liters) of fuel. It weighs over 66 tons (60 tonnes). Its armor is mostly at the front, and so, as with all tanks, it is very vulnerable to attacks from the sides or from the air.

With all that weight, the Abrams cannot be used in areas where it would get stuck or bogged down, such as marshy land. The tanks are also too big to move through thick forests or jungles. They are ineffective in mountains. In land that is criss-crossed with rivers and canals, the bridges must be able to support the weight of the tanks.

Ships

Flat-tops

The Nimitz class aircraft-carriers are the largest warships ever built. The carrier has over 6,000 personnel (crew and aircrew). Its flight deck is 364 yards (332.9 meters) long—about the length of three and half football fields.

The aircraft-carrier, or "flat-top," is at the heart of major military operations. Whenever there is a crisis, the first response is always: "Send the carriers!" Carriers support and operate aircraft that attack targets at sea, on land, and in the air.

Carriers can respond to global problems in many ways. These range from providing an important presence in peacetime to taking part in full-scale war. The carriers have an important role to play.

The flight deck of a Nimitz class aircraft-carrier is equipped with four elevators and four catapults (devices that launch the aircraft). The carrier is capable of launching one aircraft every twenty seconds.

The newest Nimitz class carrier, the USS *George H. W. Bush,* is currently being built and will enter service in 2009. The vessel will have a modernized control center with a new **radar** tower and transparent armor windows. The navigation and communications systems will be the most advanced on Earth. In fact, this ship will be the first of a whole new class of carriers.

The advanced technology that will be on board the USS *George H. W. Bush* means fewer crew are needed. This also means a smaller number of sailors are at risk.

>> What is the future?

The new Nimitz class aircraft-carriers will have a large range of countermeasures. These are systems intended to confuse the enemy or destroy anything launched against the carrier. The ship can shoot down missiles at long range in the air and destroy enemy torpedoes before they hit. Many of these systems are completely automatic. They spring to the defense of the ship as soon as enemy action is detected.

Nimitz class aircraft-carrier

Power:	2 x nuclear reactors
Length:	1,092 ft. (332.85 m)
Flight deck width:	252 ft. (76.8 m)
Beam:	134 ft. (40.84 m)
Weight displacement:	Approx. 97,000 tons full load
Speed:	30+ **knots**
Aircraft:	85
Crew:	3,184
Cost:	about $4.5 billion each

Aircraft

Nimitz class carriers usually carry the following aircraft, although this can change depending on the mission:

20 x F-14D Bombcats (fighter–bombers)
36 x F/A-18 Hornets (fighter–bombers)
8 x S-3A/B Vikings (anti-submarine warfare)
4 x E-2C Hawkeyes
(early-warning **reconnaissance**)
4 x EA-6B Prowlers (electronic warfare)

Helicopters

4 x SH-60F Seahawks
(rescue, anti-submarine, and transportation)
2 x HH-60H Seahawks
(rescue, anti-submarine, and transportation)

The new carriers will be armed with three launchers for NATO Seasparrow **surface-to-air missiles**. Seasparrow missiles have a range of 9 miles (14.5 kilometers) and are guided by radar. The carriers are also being fitted with the Raytheon Rolling Airframe missile system.

This provides short-range defense against incoming anti-ship missiles, including sea-skimming missiles. In addition, there are 20-mm 6-barreled Mk 15 **close-in weapon systems**. These have an incredible firing rate of 3,000 rounds per minute and a range of 0.9 miles (1.5 kilometers).

Virginia-class submarines

The first submarine of the new Virginia class is the USS *Virginia*. It weighs approximately 8,600 tons (7,800 tonnes) and is 371 feet (113 meters) long. It is longer than the previous Seawolf class of submarines, but it is also lighter and quicker.

The 134-member crew of the *Virginia* will be able to attack targets on the shore with Tomahawk Cruise missiles, which are highly accurate.

It will be able to conduct secret long-term surveillance (keeping watch closely) of land areas, inland waters, or other ships. It will also carry anti-submarine and anti-ship warfare, special-forces delivery and support, mine delivery, and minefield mapping (see pages 44 and 45).

The Virginia class of attack submarines outperforms any other ship under the water.

✕ Make the connection

In the early 1990s, the United States needed a new and better submarine. The new craft was needed to:

- Carry out secret strikes by launching missiles from underwater
- Engage and defeat enemy submarines
- Sink enemy ships
- Support battle groups with advanced communication equipment
- Conduct secret reconnaissance
- Monitor enemy communications
- Lay mines against enemy ships
- Launch special operations, such as search and rescue, diversionary attacks (drawing attention away), and supporting other units.

The new type of submarine is named the Virginia class.

The Typhoon class submarine is perhaps the most destructive and feared weapon ever created.

Destruction from the depths

Perhaps the single most destructive weapon ever created is the **ballistic-missile** nuclear submarine. It can silently creep up on an enemy position and, from underwater, launch nuclear missile attacks of enormous power. A single sub could destroy a country.

Typhoon–class submarines

Ballistic-missile nuclear-powered submarines of the Typhoon class are the largest submarines ever built. They are potentially the greatest single destructive weapon on the planet.

The Typhoon-class submarine is a multi-hulled vessel. This means it has five inner hulls, all placed inside a superstructure of two parallel main hulls. The surface of the superstructure is coated with sound-absorbent tiles. Its design includes features for traveling under ice and ice-breaking. The maximum diving depth is 1,312 feet (400 meters). These submarines are capable of speeds up to 12 knots when surfaced and 25 knots when under water. Typhoon-class subs are also able to stay at sea for up to 120 days.

The submarine carries twenty ballistic missiles. Each missile consists of ten independently targeting **warheads**, each with a 110-kiloton nuclear warhead. (The bomb dropped on Hiroshima, Japan, in World War II was 14.3 kilotons; see page 30.) Their range is about 5,160 miles (8,300 kilometers) and is accurate to about 1,640 feet (500 meters).

The Sea Shadow

Any weapon is more useful if an enemy cannot see it or find it. This is particularly true at sea, where there are not many places for a weapon to hide if discovered.

The Sea Shadow is an experiment in stealth technology. The vessel has been built using similar technology to stealth aircraft (see pages 38–41). It is being used in testing **automation** and **advanced information technologies**. These advances will reduce crew sizes throughout the U.S. fleet.

The Sea Shadow runs at a top speed of 10 knots and has a length and beam of roughly 164 by 69 feet (50 by 21 meters). It has a crew of ten sailors.

For many years, the Sea Shadow was a top-secret operation. More recently this secrecy has been relaxed. Originally the U.S. Navy thought it could never expect to make a much larger ship "disappear" like the B-2 stealth bomber or the F-117 can. Now the navy is more hopeful that one day it will achieve this. Until then, being able to avoid detection long enough to fire weapons or to launch and recover aircraft will prove very valuable in future conflicts.

A weird-looking ship . . . but the whole point is that no one sees it!

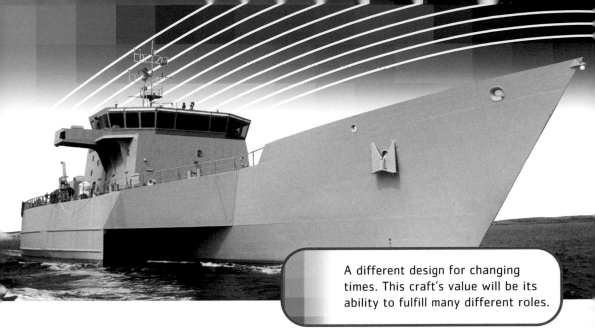

A different design for changing times. This craft's value will be its ability to fulfill many different roles.

The FSC

The United Kingdom's Royal Navy has a plan to design a warship that will eventually replace current warships. It is called the Future Surface Combatant (FSC). The FSC is still being designed, but it will have the ability to be used for all missions, from peaceful support to all-out warfare.

The FSC could be a trimaran. This means it would have three hulls. This revolutionary design feature would offer the benefits of being more stable in rough seas, more efficient in the water (having less **drag**), and allowing more deck space for weapons systems. There would also be extra space for landing helicopters on the flight deck. The greater stability offered by three hulls would allow communications equipment to be kept higher in the ship. This would improve the performance of the transmitters and receivers.

>> What is the future?

Another major technological breakthrough that navies could benefit from in the future is the use of electric **propulsion** motors. Experts believe this would be as important as the change from sail to steam. The ships would be more efficient and would operate at lower costs.

Missiles

How rockets work

Rockets work by propulsion. In simple terms, this means that the rocket is pushed forward by material spurting out of the back of it. Most rockets work by superheated gases being pushed out of the back of them. These gases form by burning fuel.

Rockets and missiles are a deadly part of every military force. Huge missiles carrying nuclear weapons can be fired into low **orbit**.

Aircraft use small missiles to destroy targets on the ground or other aircraft. Submarines rise to the surface to release larger missiles on unsuspecting targets. Even infantry soldiers can carry small missiles to shoot down threats in the air.

Recent conflicts around the world have seen an increased use of these weapons. The public has even seen pictures from cameras attached to the missiles as they fly toward a target.

This short-range LANCE missile is launched from a moving platform. An enemy will not know where attacks are coming from.

Types of missile

- *Battlefield Short-Range Ballistic Missile (BSRBM)*: Often handheld weapons with a range of less than 100 miles
- *Short-Range Ballistic Missile (SRBM)*: A range of 95–620 miles
- *Medium-Range Ballistic Missile (MRBM)*: A range of 620–1,700 miles
- *Intermediate-Range Ballistic Missile (IRBM)*: A range of 1,700–3,100 miles
- *Intercontinental Ballistic Missile (ICBM)*: A ballistic missile with a range of more than 3,100 miles. The term *ICBM* only applies to missiles fired from land.
- *Submarine-Launched Ballistic Missiles (SLBM)*: These have different ranges, although often similar to those of ICBMs.

The success of any missile system depends on the accuracy of its guidance system. Military leaders are eager to stress that these systems are so accurate that targets can be destroyed without loss of **civilian** life, even when the targets are close to civilian areas. Recent conflicts have provided much evidence of military buildings destroyed from hundreds of miles away, without any surrounding civilian buildings suffering damage.

But mistakes still happen, since the technology is not foolproof. There have been occasions when missile **batteries** have automatically targeted friendly aircraft and shot them down. Slight computer malfunctions can send missiles wildly off course with tragic results. Some people argue that human beings should not depend so much on advanced technology for protection, especially when it can go wrong.

✂ Make the connection

Rockets become weapons by adding an explosive warhead to the tip. When the rocket strikes the target, the warhead explodes. There are many advantages to using missiles as weapons:

- They can be fired from a safe distance with little risk to the user
- They can be fired with highly accurate guidance systems
- They can travel huge distances
- Different warheads can be used, depending on the target.

Cruise missiles

The Cruise is the best-known missile. In effect, it is a small jet without a pilot. It can fly up to 1,865 feet (3,000 kilometers) to a target, carrying huge warheads. The Cruise missile can also carry nuclear weapons.

Cruise missiles can cost up to $1 million each. They are an expensive way to deliver bombs, since the missile is destroyed after the bomb explodes.

Cruise missiles are excellent at avoiding detection by the enemy because they fly very low to the ground and avoid being seen by radar.

A guided missile cruiser launches a weapon of deadly accuracy.

✕ Make the connection

A Cruise missile is incredibly accurate. It flies for hundreds of miles and can hit a target the size of a car. Four completely different guidance systems make the Cruise so accurate:

- *IGS (inertial guidance system)*: The Cruise's own computer system that calculates position based on the missile's movement
- *Tercom*: This system recognizes the ground it is flying over by comparing it with a 3-D map in the missile's own database
- *GPS*: Cruise uses the Global Positioning System, a system of satellites, to pinpoint its position
- *DSMAC*: Using a camera, this system can actually find a moving target and focus in on it.

The Patriot is an unusual missile, since its main purpose is defense. Most missiles are designed to attack.

Proud Patriots

The Patriot is a missile that shoots down other missiles. It can detect, target, and then destroy an enemy missile that might be no more than 20 feet (6 meters) long and flying at incredibly high speeds.

A Patriot missile battery uses the most advanced technology. The base system launches and controls the missile. A radar antenna continuously scans the sky looking for targets. Once it detects a target, the system calculates the most effective route for the Patriot missile. It then sends the guidance information to that missile and launches it. Within three seconds, the missile is speeding at five times the speed of sound toward the enemy missile.

A different version of the Patriot contains its own computer system, allowing it to guide itself. Once in the air, this Patriot finds the target and aims for a direct hit.

The technology required to make a direct hit needs to be amazingly precise. It is like trying to hit one bullet with another bullet. These missiles, however, are going up to five times faster than a normal bullet and they are flying toward each other. The tiniest error would cause the Patriot to miss by a long way.

The successful Sidewinder

The AIM-9M Sidewinder missile is one of the most successful weapons on Earth. It has been used for many years. It has been constantly developed, and its technology has been upgraded. This has allowed it to remain a cutting-edge combination of electronics and explosive power.

The Sidewinder is a short-range air-to-air missile. This means it is launched by one aircraft to destroy another. Missiles like the Sidewinder are called smart weapons because they contain electronic systems that let them track and close in on a target.

Sidewinder AIM–9M

Length:	9.5 ft. (2.9 m)
Weight:	187 lbs. (85 kg)
Cost:	$84,000
Top speed:	**Mach** 2.5
Range:	18 mi. (29 km)

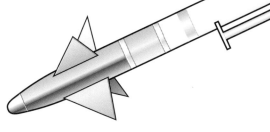

- The guidance-control computer, which calculates the missile's course

- The fins, which steer the missile. They are moved by the guidance computer like the flaps on an aircraft's wing.

- The warhead, which destroys the target

- An arming system that sets the warhead off only when it approaches the target

- A battery to provide power to the missile's electronics.

The sidewinder has eight main components

- The rocket motor, which provides power to fly the missile

- The rear wings, which lift the missile

- The heat-seeker, which detects the target

FIM-92A (Stinger)

Length:	4.9 ft. (1.5 m)
Diameter:	2.8 in. (7 cm)
Weight:	22 lbs. (10 kg)
Weight with launcher:	33.5 lbs. (15.2 kg)
Speed:	1,490 mph (2,400 km/h)
Altitude range:	Approximately 1.9 mi. (3 km)
Distance range:	Approximately 5 mi. (8 km)

Missiles from the shoulder

The Stinger missile, officially called the FIM-92A, gives infantry troops a way to deal with low-flying aircraft and helicopters. It uses an infrared heat-seeking system to lock onto the exhaust of a target's engine. It works up to a height of 11,000 feet (3,353 meters).

The Stinger is such an effective weapon for ground troops to use because:

- It is light and can be carried easily. The missile and its reusable launcher weigh only 33 pounds (15 kilograms).

- It can be operated by a single person

- The infrared heat-seeker system is very accurate

- Once the trigger is pulled, the missile does the rest. Infantry troops call this a "fire-and-forget" weapon.

In simple terms, if a target is less than 1.9 miles (3 kilometers) high and can be seen as a shape rather than a speck, the Stinger missile can hit it.

Nuclear Weapons

Even though countries have recently agreed to reduce numbers, there are still enough nuclear weapons on Earth to blow up the whole planet many times over. Without a doubt, they are the most terrifying and destructive weapons ever created.

When a nuclear bomb explodes, everything at the heart of the explosion is instantly **vaporized** by temperatures up to 540 million °F (300 million °C). This is about twenty times hotter than the core of the Sun. Moving outward from the center of the explosion, most of the injured are burned or are hit by collapsing buildings. There are many other health problems caused by exposure to the very high levels of radiation.

When the U.S. dropped a nuclear bomb on Hiroshima, Japan, in 1945, it caused terrible destruction. The bomb used was very small by today's standards.

The effects of nuclear weapons are very long term. One effect of many nuclear bombs exploding at the same time would be a nuclear winter. Huge clouds of radioactive dust would travel high up into Earth's atmosphere, blocking out the sunlight. The temperature of the planet would drop, and this would affect animals and plants. The food chain would be disrupted, causing mass extinctions (the dying out of specific life-forms).

Since 1945 a debate has raged about banning nuclear weapons. The main arguments are outlined in the box below.

For banning the bomb

- The effects last a long time— for thousands of years

- A nation may be tempted to use them against nations that do not have nuclear technology

- Such weapons cannot win wars, since any territory gained cannot be used

- Nuclear research should focus on providing energy rather than weapons

- An accident could be an enormous disaster.

Against banning the bomb

- You cannot "un-invent" things

- Because they are so powerful, having them means no one would dare use one against you

- Using a nuclear weapon shortens wars, and lives could thus be saved by ending a conflict quickly

- It is better to master the technology than to ignore it

- If governments claim to have banned the weapons, how can we be sure? What about terrorists?

Aircraft

The flying tank

The Apache attack helicopter is a revolutionary development in the history of war. Experts describe it as a flying tank. It can survive heavy attack and cause massive damage itself. Nothing creates more fear among ground forces than the appearance of the Apache, the most deadly helicopter ever flown.

The Apache has computerized flight systems that make it more agile. It is extremely strong—strong enough, in fact, to withstand brushes with trees and other obstacles. This is essential, because it allows it to fly very low. Apaches fly near the ground to sneak up on targets and avoid attack. While the construction of the Apache is similar to other helicopters, its advanced weapons put it in an entirely different class.

Fast, agile, well-protected, and very heavily armed: the Apache is a weapon you want to have on your side!

Hellfire

The Apache can carry up to sixteen Hellfire missiles. Each missile is a miniature aircraft with its own guidance computer, steering control, and propulsion system. The helicopter's radar locates a target, and the missiles zero in on it. The helicopter can simply pop up above cover, fire the missile, and immediately find cover once more. The warheads are powerful enough to cut through the thickest tank armor.

Hydra

Apaches can also use Hydra rocket launchers. Each launcher carries nineteen missiles. The rockets operate with several different warheads. They can be armed with high-power explosives or merely smoke-producing materials. In one version, the warhead releases several small bombs that separate from the rocket and fall on targets below.

Chain gun

Under the helicopter's nose is an M230 30-mm automatic cannon. This is aimed using a sophisticated computer system in the cockpit. The automatic cannon is a chain gun powered by an electric motor. Unlike a conventional machine gun (see pages 10–11), the motor rotates the chain, which slides the working parts back and forth to load, fire, extract, and eject cartridges. The gun can fire 650 rounds a minute. It uses high-explosive ammunition designed to cut through light armor.

The **sensor equipment** the Apache uses is amazing. The Apache uses a radar dome to identify the shape of anything in range. A computer compares these shapes to a database of tanks, trucks, and aircraft to identify a potential target, allowing it to recognize which vehicles are friendly, too. In addition, the Apache can avoid enemy radar scanning. If the pilots pick up any enemy radar signals, they can activate jamming systems to confuse the enemy.

With all its weapons, its armor, and its sensor equipment, the Apache attack helicopter can take on anything else on the battlefield.

Tomorrow's helicopters

Helicopters of the future could be very different if current design projects are successful.

Many military scientists are experimenting with tilt-rotor technology. Tilt-rotor aircraft can take off and land vertically (up and down), like a helicopter, and then tilt the rotors to the front and fly forward, like a normal aircraft. Tilting the rotors essentially turns them into propellers, allowing the craft to travel faster than a helicopter currently can.

The Osprey

The V-22 Osprey is a tilt-rotor aircraft. It takes off and lands like a helicopter but, once in the air, its engine can be rotated to convert the aircraft to a **turboprop** capable of flying at high speed and high altitude.

In addition to transportation, it can also be used for combat search-and-rescue missions. The rotors can also fold and the wing can rotate so that the aircraft can be stored aboard an aircraft-carrier. In keeping with most new military machines, the Osprey is very valuable because it can be used in many different roles.

The Osprey can carry 24 combat troops, or up to 19,850 pounds of internal or external cargo, at twice the speed of a helicopter.

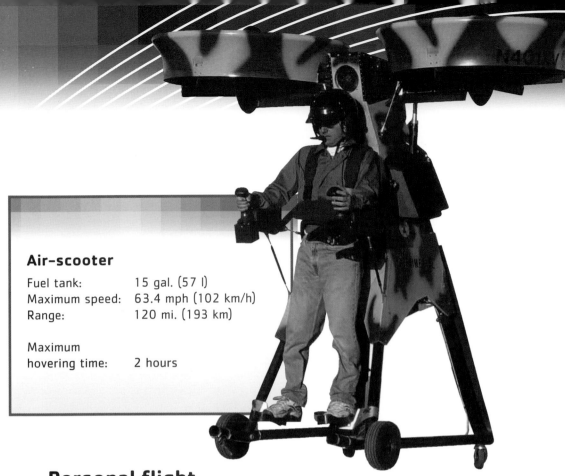

Air-scooter

Fuel tank:	15 gal. (57 l)
Maximum speed:	63.4 mph (102 km/h)
Range:	120 mi. (193 km)
Maximum hovering time:	2 hours

Personal flight

Experimental projects, such as the SoloTrek Exo-skeletor Flying Vehicle (XFV) or "Air-scooter", have also attracted the attention of the military.

Although this development looks like a gadget from a James Bond movie, it is actually at an advanced stage of the design process. In 2000 NASA successfully flew a **prototype** of this personal flight unit, powered by two covered rotors.

The trials of the Air-scooter have the potential to fulfill a decades-old dream of a device that would take the worry out of traffic jams, allow doctors to fly to emergencies, and allow troops to move easily over difficult ground.

The Air-scooter is designed to allow a standing pilot, with fans directly above his head that lift him into the sky, to achieve flight at speeds of up to 80 miles (102 kilometers) per hour for over an hour on a single tank of gasoline.

Of course, there could be many military uses for the Air-scooter. Soldiers would be able to leapfrog over minefields, cross rivers if bridges have been destroyed, or cross marshland with little effort. There could also be a use for army medics; they would be able to reach wounded troops in places where normal helicopters could not travel. Reaching the wounded quickly is an essential part of saving lives.

Invisible assassin

The F/A-22 Raptor is the world's first air-dominance fighter. It is deadly and cannot be seen at long range. It is also unmatched at close-in **dogfighting**.

With amazing precision capabilities for ground attack, the F-22 will dominate the skies over any future battlefield. The U.S. Air Force plans to build a total of 339 Raptors during the next decade to replace its fleet of F-15 Eagles. The first Raptor squadron (a unit in the air force) is scheduled to be operational in 2005.

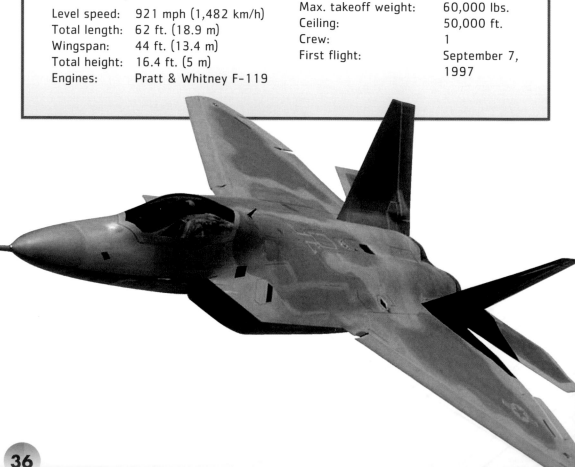

F/A 22 Raptor

Level speed:	921 mph (1,482 km/h)	Max. takeoff weight:	60,000 lbs.
Total length:	62 ft. (18.9 m)	Ceiling:	50,000 ft.
Wingspan:	44 ft. (13.4 m)	Crew:	1
Total height:	16.4 ft. (5 m)	First flight:	September 7, 1997
Engines:	Pratt & Whitney F-119		

✕ Make the connection

Many argue that there was little need for the Raptor to be built at all. The United States already has an outstanding fighter jet in the F-15. Many believe that the huge cost of developing the Raptor could have been spent on more deserving causes. Military experts disagree. They argue that only so much new technology can be bolted onto an old airframe. Stealth technology is the future of combat flying, and the F-15 is simply out-of-date in this respect. In addition, the Raptor can cover ten times more battle space than the F-15.

Cockpit

The Raptor's cockpit is both state-of-the-art and a work of art. There are six color liquid-crystal displays. These displays provide a plan view of the air and ground situation, including identifying enemy threats. The Raptor's equipment can even prioritize the targets, leaving the less threatening until last. A video camera captures every movement of the plane and pilot for later analysis.

The F-22 Raptor achieves air dominance through a skillful mixture of stealth technologies, awesome engines, agility, and highly advanced computer systems. The engines allow the Raptor to reach uncontested heights and achieve speeds unheard of by other fighters.

The Raptor's main weapons bays are packed with either six radar-guided missiles to attack other aircraft or four huge air-to-ground missiles. The F-22 also carries two heat-seeking missiles, one in each of its side weapons bays.

As a result, the Raptor can fly very high, very far, and very fast with little risk of being detected or intercepted. It can strike with confidence against targets both in the air and on the ground. The U.S. Air Force believes that it is the one aircraft that can maintain U.S. air dominance.

Stealth

Although stealth technology is now used in other areas, it was first put to use in the air. The purpose of stealth technology is to make an aircraft invisible to radar. There are two different ways to create invisibility:

- The plane can be designed so that any radar signals reflected from it are diverted away from the radar equipment that is trying to detect it

- The plane can be covered in special materials that absorb radar signals.

Stealth planes use both of these methods to help them "disappear." An "invisible aircraft" is an enormous threat, and army forces around the globe are rushing to perfect this new technology.

The Nighthawk

For about seven years, the F-117 Nighthawk had been flying without anyone even knowing it was there. Only when it was introduced to the public was its existence confirmed.

The Nighthawk has additional features that help to make the plane difficult to see:

- All the weapons are actually carried inside the body, because weapons hanging beneath a wing are easier for radar to spot. Only at the very last second are the doors opened and the weapons fired.

- The engines are hidden deep within the aircraft's wings. This makes the spinning jet blades and the engine heat harder to detect.

✂ Make the connection

Most aircraft have a rounded shape to make them **aerodynamic**. This also makes them very effective in reflecting radar. The round shape means that no matter where the radar signal hits the plane, some of the signal gets reflected back. Stealth aircraft, however, have completely flat surfaces and sharp edges. When the radar signal hits a plane built this way, the signal is shot away at an angle. In addition, surfaces on a stealth aircraft are covered so that they absorb radar energy. The overall result is that a stealth aircraft such as an F-117A looks like a small bird to a radar operator.

F-117 Nighthawk

Engines:	Two General Electric F404 engines	Weight:	52,084 lbs. (23,625 kg)
Length:	66.6 ft. (20.3 m)	Wingspan:	43.6 ft. (13.3 m)
Height:	12.5 ft. (3.8 m)	Speed:	**High subsonic**
		Range:	Unlimited with air refueling

The F-117, also known as the "Wobblin' Goblin," has had outstanding success, since it is able to get into highly dangerous environments and attack important targets with deadly accuracy. The Nighthawk has been in service in Panama, during Operation Desert Storm in the Gulf, in Kosovo, and during Operation Iraqi Freedom.

At the moment, the Nighthawk is only used for night missions. However, tests are currently evaluating the F-117 for use on daylight operations.

By the time F-117s had made 1,300 combat missions, only one had been shot down. This makes the Nighthawk the most effective attack aircraft ever.

Flying wing

The B-2 "Spirit," or stealth bomber, is the most expensive aircraft ever built. It can carry nuclear bombs across the globe, is whisper-quiet, and is nearly invisible to enemy sensors.

The B-2 bomber has a revolutionary design: it is just one big wing. This flying wing design is much more efficient than a conventional plane, since the amount of drag is greatly reduced. This helps the B-2 travel long distances in a short period of time. It can fly to anywhere on Earth at very short notice.

The B-2 can fly undetected through enemy airspace. Ideally, a stealth aircraft is able to reach and destroy targets without a shot being fired at it.

The B-2 may be a huge plane, but cutting-edge technology makes it seem smaller than a bird on radar.

The B-2's flat, slim shape and black exterior help it disappear into the night. The B-2 has very low exhaust emissions, so it does not leave a visible trail behind it.

Its engines are very quiet. They are buried inside the plane, which helps reduce the noise of the engine. The efficient aerodynamic design also helps keep the B-2 quiet, because the engines can operate at lower power settings. The sensors on heat-seeking missiles can detect hot engine exhausts, so in the B-2, all of the exhaust passes through cooling vents before flowing out of the aircraft.

✂ Make the connection

Because of incredibly high cost and relative inexperience in battle, the B-2 is a controversial weapon. While some experts claim it is the greatest military aircraft, others say the plane has major limitations. For example, they argue that stealth capabilities operate poorly in bad weather. Others argue that, as with the F-22, the cost should have been used for more important things. But just about everybody agrees it is a huge development in **aeronautic** technology. It is certainly an amazing machine.

Just like the Nighthawk, the B-2 has defenses against radar detection. The plane has a radar-absorbent surface. Parts of the plane are also covered in highly advanced radio-absorbent paint and tape. These materials are very expensive, and the U.S. Air Force has to reapply them regularly.

The second element in radar invisibility is the B-2's shape. The stealth bomber's weird shape deflects radio beams in many ways. The large, flat areas on the top and bottom of the plane are just like tilted mirrors. These flat areas deflect most radio beams away from detection stations.

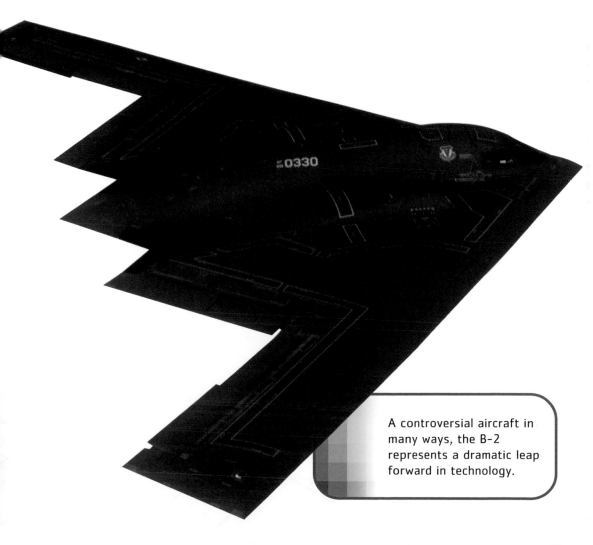

A controversial aircraft in many ways, the B-2 represents a dramatic leap forward in technology.

The versatile Joint Strike Fighter

The F-35 JSF (Joint Strike Fighter) is currently being developed and tested. By 2008 it will be in service. The idea is to replace the many different aircraft in service today with just one basic plane. Different jobs will be done by modified versions of the JSF.

The JSF is being built in three different versions:

- A normal takeoff and landing aircraft

- An aircraft for use on aircraft-carriers

- A short takeoff and vertical landing aircraft.

By developing "three-planes-in-one," money can be saved while different forces still get what they need. The U.S. Navy gets a strong plane to cope with aircraft-carrier landings. The Marine Corps get the vertical-landing capability of a Harrier Jumpjet. The U.S. Air Force gets a plane for air-to-ground missions that could measure up to the F-22 Raptor.

The JSF will cost little more than an F-16, even though it represents at least a 30 percent improvement in range, weapons, and stealth.

However, to replace the excellent aircraft already in service, the JSF must be both technologically superior and economical at the same time.

And its technology is certainly awesome:

Stealth

The JSF has many of the stealth features used by the Nighthawk and the Raptor. It is coated with radar-reflective materials and has flat surfaces to increase radar resistance (see pages 38–39). As a result, the JSF can get through missile defense systems to destroy targets with less chance of being spotted.

Firepower

The different versions of the JSF carry a wide range of cutting-edge weapons. These are carried in bays located in front of the landing gear. A JSF can be armed with Sidewinder missiles, Storm Shadow Cruise missiles, guided bombs, and several other highly accurate and deadly weapons.

Electronics

The radar systems for the JSF are being redesigned to make them more sensitive when searching for targets and to give off a signal less likely to be spotted. The pilot has the option of guiding weapons from the aircraft or letting the missiles guide themselves.

Computer systems always ensure that the aircraft can deliver maximum power at any speed or height.

It is the vertical takeoff version of the JSF that is causing the most excitement. Never before has a fighter been able to take off in this way, hover in the air, and fly at **supersonic** speeds. This is one of the reasons why the JSF is known as "the plane for all occasions."

The development of the JSF is a triumph for international relations and cooperation. The United States and the United Kingdom are the most high-profile partners, but other countries, including Italy, Turkey, Australia, Canada, the Netherlands, Denmark, and Norway, have all played a part in the fighter's development.

The ability to perform many different roles and functions is a crucial requirement of current cutting-edge technology.

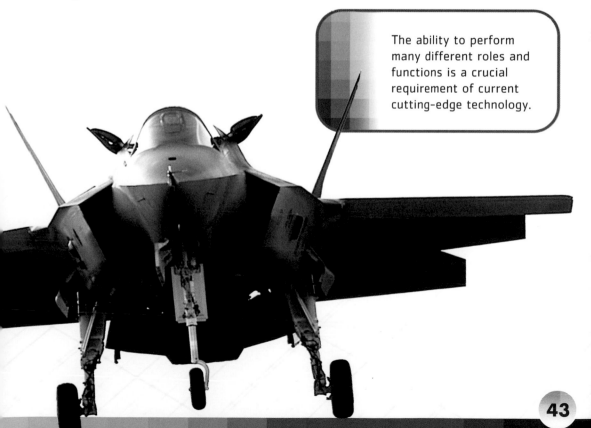

Landmines

Tread carefully

Landmines are cheap weapons that can be used effectively over large areas to prevent enemy movement in that region.

Anti-personnel mines come in three basic types:

- Blast mines: These are the most common type, buried just below the surface. They explode instantly when stepped on. Quite often they do not actually kill, but cause horrific injuries to the lower half of the body.

- Bounding mines: A small part of this type of mine sticks up above the surface. This means the mine can be triggered by stepping on it or by stepping on a tripwire attached to it. When activated the mine shoots about 3.3 feet (1 meter) in the air before exploding. Victims rarely survive.

- Fragmentation mines: These mines release bomb fragments in all directions. They are deadly at close range, but can also cause injury to people up to 656 feet (200 meters) away.

Landmines designed to destroy vehicles are basically blast mines, only with a much bigger explosive charge than anti-personnel mines. They are designed to let a person walk on them without exploding, since they are only intended for bigger targets.

This anti-personnel mine was discovered near Sarajevo after the Balkans conflict. The Ottawa Convention signed in 1997 bans the use and production of landmines. However, the millions of mines still in the ground will continue to claim civilian lives.

The Asian country of Afghanistan has an estimated 10 million landmines still buried in its soil. As a result, more than 400,000 people have been killed or injured by landmines since 1991.

Buried killers

The use of landmines causes much argument and debate. There are many who believe they should be completely banned. Critics argue that landmines continue to take the lives of civilians long after any conflict has finished.

Landmines can remain active for years. They are also difficult and dangerous to remove, which is why many armies simply do not bother. They just leave them in the ground.

It is estimated that a staggering 110 million mines are still silently waiting to claim their victims. Landmines kill 26,000 people a year and seriously injure tens of thousands more. Twenty-five countries have been declared in a state of crisis because of landmines. More worryingly, for every landmine cleared today, another twenty are still being laid somewhere in the world.

Arms manufacturers have responded by producing "smart" landmines, which switch themselves off after a certain period of time. But this does not satisfy the many people and organizations that are actively campaigning for production to be banned.

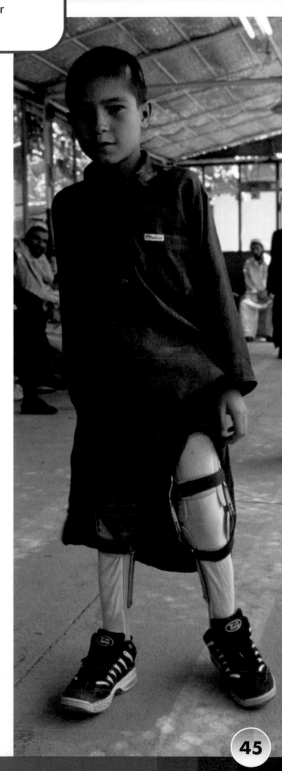

Artillery

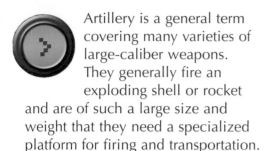

Artillery is a general term covering many varieties of large-caliber weapons. They generally fire an exploding shell or rocket and are of such a large size and weight that they need a specialized platform for firing and transportation.

Artillery types

The types of artillery are distinguished by the **trajectory** of the shells they fire. Cannons (such as infantry support guns or the guns on a ship) are usually fired when the barrel is at a low angle. Mortars fire at a very high angle. Howitzers are capable of both high- and low-angle fire.

Artillery is generally used to support troops in ground battles. The big guns can pound away at enemy positions from a safe distance before troops advance on the enemy. Artillery can also be called upon when troops are in trouble, by directing fire upon an enemy that is approaching.

Self-propelled artillery vehicles look similar to tanks, but the gun they carry is much bigger. These vehicles are not designed for direct combat, since they have little or no armor. They are used for long-range attack. Their tanklike appearance just makes it easier for them to be moved around.

A U.S. M110 howitzer in action during the Gulf War.

The FH2000 Field Howitzer is generally regarded as the most devastating and technologically advanced artillery weapon in use by any military force.

The heavy stuff

The FH2000 field howitzer is considered the best artillery weapon around. It is easier to operate, has more advanced technology, a longer range, and more deadly firepower than any of its competitors.

The FH2000 has electronic circuitry that operates the gun at the touch of a button. The power unit means the gun has self-propelled capabilities. This means it can be set up and ready to fire in less than two minutes by a crew of six people. It is important for artillery units to move around as much as possible, so that enemy artillery cannot find them.

The FH2000 has a maximum range of 25 miles (40 kilometers). The advanced automated technology helps achieve this range. The "flick-rammer," for example, is a device that automatically flicks and rams the shells into the barrel. The gun can fire three rounds within twenty seconds, which is amazingly fast, considering the size of the shells.

The advanced design of the gun means that it is quick and simple to maintain. The gun was also designed to be used with equipment that already existed, such as towing vehicles and ammunition. This means it is relatively cheap to operate.

Laser Technology

Laser technology is no longer something that only exists in science-fiction movies. Lasers are now used everyday in CD and DVD players, eye surgery, measuring equipment, and much more. But will we ever see them being used as weapons?

Chemical lasers produce a light beam by using a chemical reaction. However, a lot of chemicals are needed, and the machinery required to produce the laser is enormous.

This means that these lasers are not very practical when used as weapons. To make lasers smaller in size, a great amount of research is being done with solid-state lasers. These use electricity to generate a beam. At the moment, scientists are trying to reduce the size of one laser so that it will fit into a C-130 cargo plane.

Laser technology is being developed into a whole new class of weapon.

✕ Make the connection

A laser is produced by "exciting" the atoms in a substance in a very controlled manner until they give out particles of light. This light can then be channeled so that all the light particles travel in the same direction at the same time with the same wavelength. This allows the beam of light to travel huge distances with almost no spreading out or loss of intensity.

Once fully developed, solid-state lasers could shoot down mortars and artillery shells in flight and explode ammunition in enemy storage. They could even wipe out ballistic missiles hundreds of miles away. Lasers would strike with incredible speed and are simple to target.

Compared to chemical lasers now, solid-state lasers would be relatively compact and efficient. They might even get power running from a Jeep's engine or an Air Force F-16.

Solid-state lasers are certainly deadly. In a recent demonstration, a test-fired laser shot out 400 pulses of light in two seconds, drilling through 1 inch (2.5 centimeters) of steel in the process.

≫ What is the future?

Contrary to what we imagine from science fiction, future weapons using lasers will not have visible streams of light that make an odd sound. Instead, the laser would not be seen or heard: targets will simply explode. Soldiers will not point and shoot the lasers, either, because the targets will probably be moving too fast for a human to respond to. At the moment, the "ray-gun" is still a long way off. The smallest laser technology to date is about the size of a small jetliner.

Star Wars

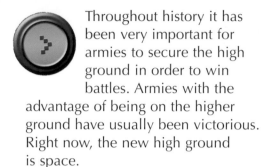

Throughout history it has been very important for armies to secure the high ground in order to win battles. Armies with the advantage of being on the higher ground have usually been victorious. Right now, the new high ground is space.

In order to defeat a nuclear attack, the United States has been developing a missile defense system in space for at least twenty years. This involves the development of laser weapons that would orbit Earth to shoot down ballistic missiles in flight. The project came to be known as Star Wars.

There is a possibility of the United States developing a fifth military organization, perhaps even called Space Force.

The Star Wars idea was criticized by many for its huge costs, doubts that it would work properly and effectively, and concerns that it would unsettle the nuclear balance of power in the world. If it worked, one country would have a significant military advantage that would make others very nervous. The arguments still go on about whether such a system is needed, but the technology continues to be developed. At the moment, between $4 and 6 billion is being spent on it every year.

>> What is the future?

There are several kinds of space weapon currently under development:

- *Chemical lasers*: There are three types of chemical laser being developed. These all involve mixing chemicals inside the weapons platform to create a laser beam.

- *Particle beams*: The energy blasts fired from a particle-beam weapon would enter into the target's materials, heating the atoms that make it up. The sharp increase in the target's temperature would quickly cause it to explode.

- *Military space planes*: A project known as the X-33 is an attempt to improve upon the Space Shuttle. It is a plane that can simply fly into space without the need for huge fuel tanks that can only be used once.

Satellite spying technology has been very effective. Every movement of enemy troops can be observed from space. The next frontier in space is much more adventurous: satellite weapons systems to shoot down nuclear missiles.

Many argue that a shield that could shoot down nuclear missiles in the air is a great development. They believe that if such a shield could prevent a nuclear attack from happening, then the nuclear threat would effectively be ended. Others believe that there is not a technological fix to the complex relationships between countries, and that even more complex weapons will only mean increased danger.

Will outer space be the battlefield for the cutting-edge weapons of the future?

Fighting the Future

Most outstanding inventions begin as someone's crazy idea. The concepts on these two pages are still little more than ideas. But one day, maybe . . .

Bioelectronical weapons

Scientists have developed a generator to produce high-frequency radiation. It was designed to kill insects by paralyzing their nervous systems. Early tests have been successful, and there is no reason why the technology cannot be applied to other living things.

"Rods from God"

Known as the "Rods from God" idea, this weapon would consist of a satellite in orbit stocked with metal rods about 20 feet (6 meters) long and 1 foot (30.5 centimeters) thick. These would be guided by satellites to targets anywhere on Earth in minutes. It is thought they would be accurate to within 25 feet (7.6 meters) and would hit Earth at speeds over 12,000 feet (3,657 meters) per second.

This is enough to destroy even hardened concrete bunkers buried underground. No explosives would even be needed. The speed and weight of the rods would cause all the damage needed.

Meteorological weapons

Scientists have had some success producing artificial weather conditions in laboratories. The research has been based around changing the electric charge of the air. Hard rains, droughts, or blizzards could cause very serious damage to an enemy. Imagine the power of a weapon that could harness the power of the weather.

Tectonic weapons

Artificial earthquakes could be used in the future as a weapon to destroy cities and towns. Scientists have an excellent understanding of the way Earth is constructed, and a weapon could be designed to use this knowledge. There are some who even believe that such a weapon already exists, and that some "real" earthquakes have actually been testing this technology.

Solar weapons

In the 3rd century B.C.E., Greek mathematician Archimedes supposedly burned the Roman fleet with the help of mirrors and the Sun. Lens technology is highly advanced today, and weapons could be developed to make use of this. Unfortunately a rain shower would be the same as running out of ammunition!

Visual stealth

Stealth technology makes aircraft invisible to radar, but not to the human eye. Aircraft that are invisible to the human eye in daylight would be a huge advantage. A project called Chameleon is developing such technology by using fiber-optic lighting systems to reduce the contrast between an aircraft and the sky. The idea is an aircraft that gives off light to blend in with the background.

Pain beams

A weapon is being researched to transmit a narrow beam of electromagnetic energy to heat the skin, but without causing any permanent damage. The pain would be unbearable, causing the victim to pass out. A long-range version could knock out populated areas, allowing troops to move in.

Water power

Riot police already use waterjets to control crowds. A jet with higher power would make a deadly weapon. Perhaps one day water pistols really will be something to fear.

It is nice to imagine a future without weapons, but this is unlikely. What is certain is that future weapons will be very different from those we use today.

Glossary

advanced information technology cutting-edge computer systems

aerodynamic something designed to cut through air with minimal wind resistance

aeronautics to do with travel through the air

Allies in World War II, countries working together that included the U.S., UK, France, the Soviet Union, and China

ammunition objects fired from guns, cannons, mortars, etc.

armament weapons and supplies with which a military unit is equipped

automation automatic operation or control of equipment

ballistic a ballistic missile travels long distances and cannot be controlled once launched. Ballistics is the study of how objects move when fired into the air.

battery site of one or more pieces of artillery

bayonet long, sharp blade attached to the end of a rifle

beam widest part of a ship

belt link clip that holds bullets together so they can be fed quickly through a machine gun

caliber diameter of bullets or shells

camouflage to make something difficult to see because it looks similar to its surroundings

cartridge metal case containing the explosive charge for a gun

chain gun type of machine gun that uses an external source of power, rather than recoil, to reload the weapon

civilian not a member of the armed forces

close-in weapon system weapons designed for close-range combat

contaminated made dirty or polluted by chemicals

dogfighting fighting between military aircraft

drag when air pushes back at an object, slowing it down

fire control system technology that controls the rate of fire and targeting choice of weapons

flotation ability of a track to remain on top of a soft surface

guerrilla member of a military group that is not official and usually wishes to change the political situation

high subsonic just below the speed of sound

infantrymen soldier trained to fight on foot

knot unit for measuring the speed of ships: 1 knot = 1.15 mph, or 1.85 km/h

Mach speed of sound. Mach 2 is twice the speed of sound.

magazine part of a gun that holds bullets

muzzle end of a gun barrel

optics related to vision

orbit path an object takes as it revolves around a planet

propulsion force that pushes something forward

prototype first form of something new, made before it is produced in larger numbers

radar way of detecting things over great distances

radiation energy that is transmitted as invisible rays

recoil sudden backward movement of a gun when fired

reconnaissance collecting information about an enemy

round bullet

sensor equipment machines with the purpose of detecting things

skate mount platform that moves quickly in different directions

supersonic faster than the speed of sound

surface–to–air missiles missiles fired from the ground at airborne targets

suspension system that protects a vehicle from bumps and shocks as it moves

tactic plan or method for achieving something

thermal viewer device that enables someone to see in the dark by detecting the heat that objects give off

trajectory path that a missile or bullet takes

tread pattern on a tire that helps it to grip a surface

turboprop jet engine used to drive a propeller

turret heavily armed, rotating part of a tank that contains the main gun

vaporize converted into gas; reduced to microscopic particles

warhead front part of a bomb or missile that explodes

Further Resources

Fowler, Will. *Modern Weapons and Warfare*. New York: Lorenz, 2000.

Hansen, Ole Steen. *Modern Military Aircraft*. New York: Crabtree, 2003.

Herbst, Judith. *The History of Weapons*. Minneapolis: Lerner, 2005.

Nardo, Don. *Weapons and Warfare*. San Diego: Lucent, 2004.

Wolny, Philip. *Weapons Satellites*. New York: Rosen, 2003.

Index